I0731970

Words of Wisdom

Sir, my concern is not whether God is on our side; my greatest concern is to be on God's side, for God is always right.

Abraham Lincoln

**He who learns
must suffer.
And even in our sleep
pain that cannot forget
falls drop by drop upon
the heart, and in
our own despair,
against our will,
comes wisdom to us by
the awful
grace of God.**

Aeschylus

No act of kindness,
no matter
how small,
is ever wasted.

Aesop

To err is human; to forgive, divine.

Alexander Pope

There is only one corner of the universe you can be certain of improving, and that's your own self.

Aldous Huxley

Change will not come if we wait for some other person or some other time. We are the ones we've been waiting for. We are the change that we seek.

Barack Obama

Truth is everybody is going to hurt you: you just gotta find the ones worth suffering for.

Bob Marley

Your vision
will become clear
only when you can
look into your own
heart.
Who looks outside,
dreams;
who looks inside,
awakes.

Carl Jung

Have a heart that never hardens, and a temper that never tires, and a touch that never hurts.

Charles Dickens

No one should fear
to undertake
any task
in the name of
our Saviour,
if it is just and
if the intention
is purely for His holy
service.

Christopher Columbus

I never saw a wild thing sorry for itself.
A small bird
will drop frozen dead
from a bough
without
ever having felt sorry
for itself.

D. H. Lawrence

Life is ours to be spent, not to be saved.

D. H. Lawrence

If you want others to be happy, practice compassion. If you want to be happy, practice compassion.

Dalai Lama

Inaction breeds doubt and fear. Action breeds confidence and courage. If you want to conquer fear, do not sit home and think about it. Go out and get busy.

Dale Carnegie

The most disadvantageous peace is better than the most just war.

Desiderius Erasmus

In a rich man's house there is no place to spit but his face.

Diogenes

Never give a sword to a man who can't dance.

Confucius

With the new day comes new strength and new thoughts.

Eleanor Roosevelt

The greatest pleasure of life is love.

Euripides

Silence is the sleep that nourishes wisdom.

Francis Bacon

Hope is a good breakfast, but it is a bad supper.

Francis Bacon

Vitality shows in not only the ability to persist but the ability to start over.

F. Scott Fitzgerald

The only thing we have to fear is fear itself.

Franklin D. Roosevelt

Youth is the best time to be rich, and the best time to be poor.

Euripides

Only the wisest and stupidest of men never change.

Confucius

There is nothing noble in being superior to your fellow men. True nobility lies in being superior to your former self.

Ernest Hemingway

A woman is like a tea bag - you can't tell how strong she is until you put her in hot water.

Eleanor Roosevelt

Love is anterior
to life,
posterior to death,
initial of creation,
and
the exponent of
breath.

Emily Dickinson

It's not what happens to you, but how you react to it that matters.

Epictetus

**It is impossible
to live a pleasant life
without living wisely
and well and justly.
And it is impossible
to live wisely
and well and justly
without living
a pleasant life.**

Epicurus

Passion makes idiots of the cleverest men, and makes the biggest idiots clever.

Francois de La Rochefoucauld

We cannot teach people anything; we can only help them discover it within themselves.

Galileo Galilei

There is
more wisdom
in your body
than
in your deepest
philosophy.

Friedrich Nietzsche

We don't stop playing because we grow old; we grow old because we stop playing.

George Bernard Shaw

But what we call our despair is often only the painful eagerness of unfed hope.

George Eliot

Happiness can exist only in acceptance.

George Orwell

Life is
what we make it,
always has been,
always will be.

Grandma Moses

Humor

is

reason

gone mad.

Groucho Marx

Cynicism
is
humor
in ill health.

H. G. Wells

Never look back unless you are planning to go that way.

Henry David Thoreau

Failure is simply the opportunity to begin again, this time more intelligently.

Henry Ford

If you do not expect the unexpected you will not find it, for it is not to be reached by search or trail.

Heraclitus

The one thing
we can never
get enough of
is love.
And the one thing
we never give enough
is love.

Henry Miller

Everything in excess is opposed to nature.

Hippocrates

What is art? Nature concentrated.

Honore de Balzac

Happiness is not an ideal of reason, but of imagination.

Immanuel Kant

The saddest aspect of life right now is that science gathers knowledge faster than society gathers wisdom.

Isaac Asimov

In the absence

of

any other proof,

the thumb alone

would convince me

of

God's existence.

Isaac Newton

We build too many walls and not enough bridges.

Isaac Newton

**It takes
a great deal
of bravery
to stand up
to our enemies,
but just as much to
stand up
to our friends.**

J.K. Rowling

Thank You

We hope you enjoyed our book.

As a small family company, your feedback is very important to us.

Please let us know how you like our book at:

happylife.presshouse@gmail.com

www.ingramcontent.com/pod-product-compliance
Lightning Source LLC
Chambersburg PA
CBHW070410200726
48294CB00003B/1147
* 9 7 8 1 8 0 3 8 3 2 2 0 3 *